Petals of Life

Unfolding the Beauty of Growth and Resilience

Dr. Sanam Vaseem Shaikh

BookLeaf Publishing

India | USA | UK

Made with ❤ on the BookLeaf Publishing Platform
www.bookleafpub.in
www.bookleafpub.com

To my beloved husband, whose unwavering support and constant encouragement have been the pillars of my strength. You've always believed in me, even when I doubted myself, and pushed me to reach beyond what I thought was possible. To my dear brother and bhabhi, whose love and warmth have always surrounded me with a sense of belonging and security. To my mummy and di, whose wisdom, love and sacrifices have shaped the very core of who I am. To my little munchkins – Shaan, Amaan and Arfa – your innocent laughter and pure hearts fill my life with endless joy and remind me every day of the beauty in simple moments. And to Ammi and Abba, who now shine from heaven, your love still guides me in ways words cannot express. This book is a small token of my gratitude to each of you, who have touched my life in the most profound ways. You are my inspiration, my strength and the reason I keep moving forward with a heart full of love and hope.

Acknowledgements

"A journey of a thousand miles begins with a single step." – Lao Tzu

This book, Petals of Life, is not just a collection of poems; it is the result of countless steps, guided by the love, encouragement and unwavering support of many extraordinary people. First and foremost, my deepest gratitude goes to my husband, Mr. Vaseem Shaikh. An engineer and the pillar of my life, his constant belief in me, patience and love have empowered me to chase my dreams and never give up. To my brother, Mr. Shamshi Mulla and my bhabhi, Ms. Muzdan Mulla, whose love and trust have been a constant source of strength. To my ever-supportive mummy, Ms. Hasina Shaikh, and di, Ms. Feeroza Shaikh, whose sacrifices and care have shaped the person I am today. And to my little munchkins, Shaan, Amaan, and Arfa – your smiles and joy light up my world in ways words can never express.

A heartfelt thank you to my guiding angel, Ms. Shabana Coatwala. Your kindness and wisdom have illuminated my path and helped me believe in myself even during the darkest moments. To my unwavering support system, Ms. Minaz Baig, and my partner in crime, Ms. Rahila Mulla – your friendship has been my rock, turning challenges into memorable moments. To my brilliant, ever-shining friends – Ms. Nusrat Azmi, Ms. Hawabi Barmare, Ms. Mubashira Shaikh, Ms. Tairin Khan and Ms. Huda Ansari (my younger version) – your warmth, love and support have been a light in my life.

I am deeply thankful to my advisors – Ms. Zohra Sakrekar, Ms. Suvarna Parab, Ms. Hafsa Usmani, Ms. Reshma Naik, Ms. Momna Rauf, Ms. Anjula Singh and my staff – for your invaluable guidance and endless encouragement, which have nurtured my writing journey. A special mention to my childhood friend, Ms. Subi Khatib, for being there through every twist and turn of life, filling it with laughter and cherished memories.

To my beloved Ammi and Abba, the very souls of my heart, whose love continues to guide me from beyond. And to my Phuppy, Mrs. Rashida Kazi, whose encouragement ignited the spark of writing within me – your memory lives on with every word I write.

My sincere thanks to Principal Ms. Saba Patel and the entire teaching and non-teaching staff, whose encouragement has shaped me both personally and professionally. Your belief in me has been the wind beneath my wings.

Lastly, I extend my heartfelt thanks to Meena Madam for her unwavering belief in me, her guidance and her invaluable support throughout my creative journey.

I am also deeply grateful to BookLeaf Publishing, whose platform has given life to this dream, helping me bring my words to the world. Your support has been vital in transforming this vision into reality.

Each of you has played a pivotal role in bringing Petals of Life to fruition, and for that, I am eternally thankful. This book is not just mine – it is a reflection of the love, support and inspiration each of you has so generously shared with me.

Preface

Petals of Life is a collection of poems inspired by the beautiful, fleeting moments that make up our journey through life. Each poem reflects the emotions, struggles, joys and reflections that we experience along the way. Life, like a blooming flower, is a delicate balance of light and shadow, and through these verses, I have sought to capture its essence – its triumphs, its heartaches and its quiet, unspoken beauty.

This book is a tribute to the people who have touched my life in profound ways, and I hope these poems resonate with those who have ever sought meaning in the simple moments and feelings that define our lives. Thank you for joining me in this celebration of life's petals.

Ammi

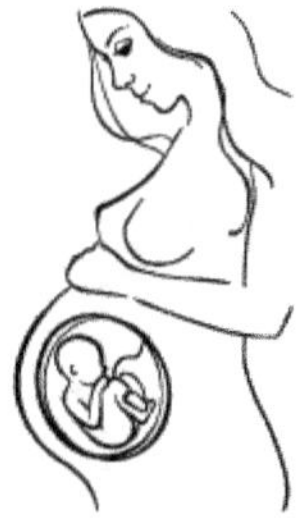

Wished her to be here,
To enjoy the moment of becoming Nani,
The joy of having a granddaughter,
The occasion of enjoying being a granny.
Wished her to be here,
By my side for logging,
In the dilemma of pain,
To be there with me when I needed her much.
Wished her to be here,
To take me along with her,
To reset me in her arms,
To teach me lessons of Motherhood.
Wished her to be here,
Just here with me during this phase
But Alas! I can just wish
I can only miss.

Aroma of Maa

When I am alone,
I miss you.
When I'm in need,
I miss you
When everybody is around me,
Still I miss you
When I'm in pain,
I miss you
When I'm happy,
I miss you
I really do
I need you
I want you
But all is futile
Our relationship was beyond mother and
daughter
Our relationship was about being the best of
buddies.

Lost Soul

The depth of insight is hidden
What I thought to be forgotten
Never went away from me
Was concealed in my soul

Past whispers in the chambers of my heart
Pain etches the memories untold
Secrets are buried in the shadows of erstwhile
Trying to wrap everything meanwhile.

Like dust in the air, it slips away
But never eradicated to betray
It exists within me, from dawn to dusk
Covering the mind in a coconut husk

Life persists, humans exist and exile
Nostalgia of the past retains in style
Concealed as a silent observer
The heart never stops to reveal

Rhythm of Dawn

As the alarm raised its beep
I see the clock and rest for five minutes
When the minutes passed don't know
When I got up, it was 7.10 oh no!

Already late by ten minutes
How to make for the commute
Train won't wait for me
Buses have their timing to come
Cabs are too demanding

Strutting seems the only source
But gosh my office is at shore
I can't make it in an hour
The traffic seemed to be a conspirer

Making me late to office
Just ten minutes of snoring
Led me twenty minutes far from my routine
Promised to keep myself ready the next day

The day comes, and I'm the same as usual.

The Seatmate's Story

Who are you and why you sit here
Sure, you are new in this compartment
Or are you unaware of the rule
Whatever the case be
At once empty the place

The perplexed new commuter urged
Laying a claim to the seat that's not yours
Don't you think is absolutely wrong
Why so much havoc, until your friend's here

She didn't get the place to sit
As by the time they finish altercation
Bestie has approached and rested her being
It amazed the unseasoned bird

No other was so concerned to make her
console
Nor someone came to argue with her
When the destination arrived
A kind soul resonated,
Don't dwell in between the seatmate's hole.

Ant

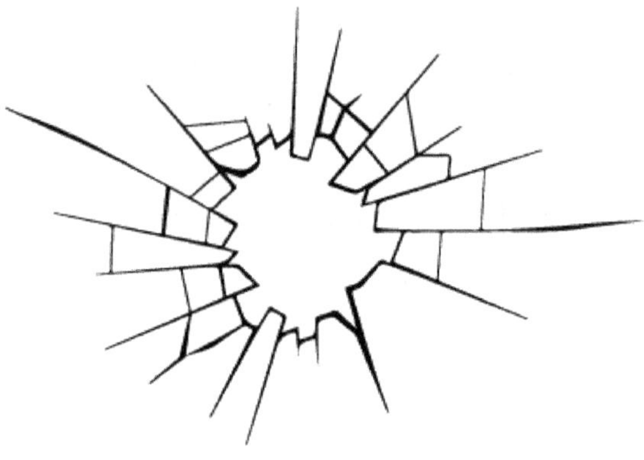

Lilliputian, tiny and thin creature
They make their way so deep
Having stings to bite you
No matter how huge are you

Heard stories of the ant and elephant in
childhood
Was delighted with the wisdom it persists
A huge animal was brought down
Just with the wee thought of young one

The figure has nothing to do with whether big
or small

What matters the most is your courage to do
If you are determined to pursue
No matter what incident occurs

So diminutive yet so powerful
Holy book too mentions its unity
So if you want to win, be careful
Be in teams and act as a community

Door

Not a day passes without me entering your life.
I'm the bond that unites you,
Bringing you closer to those who matter.
Without me, you'd be lost in ambiguity.
Rough and tough, a necessity in your life,
With me, you feel safe and secure.
Your loved ones are cherished and kept safe,
Offering comfort after all your busy moments.
Filthy at times, yet often spotless,
The décor on me reflects your status,
Making your space more attractive and glamorous,

Revealing your persona, vibrant and eminent.
Believe it or not, I'm your secret keeper,
What happens after I close, no one knows.
Guessing me wasn't hard, was it?
I'm the one who unlocks your happiness.

Abba

He was a fighter
Yes, you heard it right
He was a real-life fighter
Don't mix him with an Army man
Nope he wasn't even a Navy man
He was a man with Substance
He was the one to make me better
He fought for me at every juncture
He was reluctant to marry her daughter
Unless she is self-dependant
He was there for me as a Mother
When My Mom left for heavenly abode

The Prime Mover

As an infant, fell in love with my mother
Then thought, who gave her so much
patience?
As a child, my father became my role model
Inquired myself, who gave him so much
determination.
As a student, the intelligence of all my
teachers
Mesmerised me with the igniting soul
As a young girl, fell for my smart brother
Was wondering from where he got so much
zeal?
As a woman, got a very down-to-earth hubby

Still in awe to get such a kind gentleman
The softness of my mother-in-law
Made me ponder His Mercy
The humility of my sister-in-law
Managed to uphold my persona
The perfection of someone near
Contrived me to the blessings which I have
My friends shaped my optimism
Meena madam's kind gesture
Brought the world of literature into the
ballpark
Everyone and each one's qualities
Bond me to admire Almighty
For in each one, I find the resplendent and
bounty of Him
Yes, you got it right
And I fall in Love with the creator of
Universe

Realm of Freshness

Men O Men!
You remain the same
The arrogance and tantrums
Are characteristic traits

Women O Women!
A symbol of love
A mercy of fathom
Above all the sarcasm

You are epic of all
You are a role model for all
You are fragrance in the situation of stiffness
You are alleviation in the circumstances of
firmness

Love defines her
Affection makes her more pure
Tenderness is an attribute of her nature
Devotion makes her more subtle

The music of melody I am
For I am a woman with infinite divine

Eternal Love

The girl with sparkling eyes
Gazed at my arrival with a content heart
How are you? I, with a hesitant voice, utter
As you have left when we last met, replied she
Our departure has left a deep scar on my
heart
Even it was not easy on my part
I have always longed to be your better half

The past has gone now; we are liberated from all the cliff
Henceforth, we can dwell in free air
Neither are you a slave here
Nor am I a Princess of Palace
Our love has reached tranquillity
Extinction is not annihilation
It's the inception of our distinct fascination
Precisely, you're right
As our love will be imperishable

Born Victorious

An angel is born and blessed
Yes, you are an angel!
God's own creation
Then why the silly comparison
This women's day
I raised myself above all the competition
Don't forget when Adam was alone
God didn't create another man
He created You (The Woman)
He has empowered you with everything
So why the hell do you compete with a
dependent soul
Don't ever imagine yourself as inferior or
subordinate
You are the person above all the race

You are an entity of a powerful soul
You are the maker of the Patriarchal Society
Stop ignoring yourself
Start loving your being
Realise your worth
And march ahead.

Is stress a blessing?

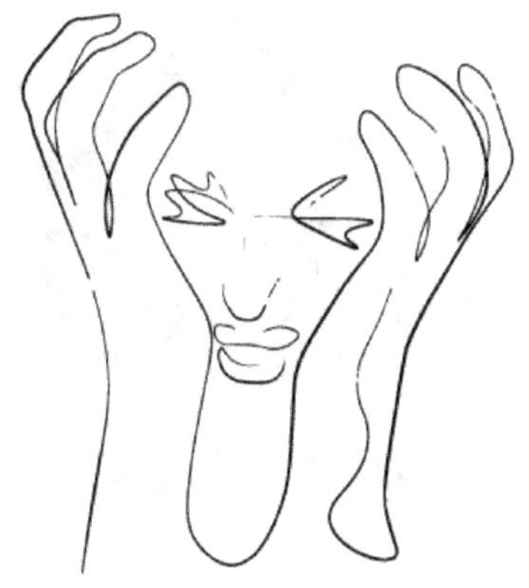

The life has given a big wave
The storm has taken all its hay
Happiness vanished within a fraction of the
ray
The pouring rain messed up the entire bay

What if even I was dead
I'm alive as My God wished
Then why mourn on the thing of the past
Let's turn the stress into opportunity

O yes! Stress can be a real blessing
It gives you time to ponder on your being

Beauty of Togetherness

Love is the soul of life
And I have found life in you
You have made me your wife
And I have found solace in you

Tenderness is the necessity of the spirit
And I have found that spirit in you
You have made me your fillet
And I have found baguette in you

Devotion is the key to marriage
And I have found that key in you
You have made me your courage
And I have found strength in you

Fidelity is the skeleton of espousal
And I have found that essence in you
You have made me your soulmate.
And I have found a confidante in you

Contemplation

Still feel to be in the arms of Ammi
Sometimes awakened by the voice of Abba
The hours of massaging hair
The showers of blessings bestowed at
midnight

The nights' sounds seemed to be scary and
alien
As now can't see the face of soothing angels
They were the source of inspiration
They still are my biggest contemplation.

As the nights fall, the serenity enthrals me
No one to see the tears nor the sobbed eyes
It gives me cherished time to lie down and
think
The adoration and admiration of my life

As the night darkened with an intensity of
shades
So, my heart peeps with the loneliness of
being left
How could they? The frequent question I
asked
My heart soothed me and replied, It's God's
will!!

The frequent shrill of any sound
Doesn't scare me now
A girl so protected and preserved seems
forlorn
Happiness and exhilaration search for their
meaning in her life.

Universe of Love

Music is felt, not sung
Lyrics are made not written
Same way, love is just love, not lust
Infatuation, obsession and passion
Can never be termed symptoms of affection
Pure love is one that doesn't ask for sacrifices
It's a form of love where you give your cent
per cent
You don't ask your partner for give-and-take
It's a relationship built on trust and care
It's said that as you grow old, you get mature
But the feeling of being loved is like old wine
The more you spend time with each other

The more understanding and compassion you
gain
I'm blessed as I have got a man
Who is a monogamist with a golden heart
You are my life partner; you are my valentine
May you be blessed with a long and healthy
life forever.

The First Time

Please put a dot, as it takes time to vanish,
'Sir, be proud you're voting, not wiping it
out', I cherish.
'Madam, I've practised responsibility since I
was 18',
The other said, 'Darken it, make it more
serene'.
With a smile on her face, the OPO asked,
'Oh, congratulations! Is it your first time,
unmasked'?
Cheeks full of blush, the girl nodded with
grace,
'Yes, I'll post on Facebook, Snapchat and
embrace'.
'You see, it's a pleasure to share with my
friends',

The OPO, curious, asked, 'How many
followers to send'?
The girl with a veil, her voice soft and light,
'Not more than 1.5', she said, keeping it tight.
She laughed, proud of the humble start,
'It's just the beginning', whispered her heart.

The Little Munchkins

A class filled with little munchkins,
Sitting at desks with mischievous eyes,
Eager to untangle all that's taught,
Breaks are not enough – eating is secondary
to gossiping's ties.
Teachers call them students, sometimes wards
and often pupils,
Their innocent words make the class vibrant,
so full.
Their intelligence reveals an inquisitive spirit,
Always making things simple, they never quit.
We can learn so much from them,
They help us revive the past, like a timeless
gem.

Courage

Shouting, yelling and throwing tantrums
Are not the true elements of courage.
Patience, calmness and sensitivity,
Indeed, reveal your inner traits.
Coping with stress,
Enduring moments of distress,
Standing against selfishness,
Personifies the real essence of courage.
True courage lies in the heart's resilience,
In facing challenges with grace and stillness.
It's found in the quiet strength of a soul,
Who rises, no matter how life takes its toll.
Be a compassionate soul,
Lead a life of purity,
For the truest form of courage
Is found in love, kindness and humility.

Glorification of Soul

Emancipation of women is not about fashion
It's neither confined to freedom of choice
The sanctification of women lies in thinking
big
It lies in searching for their true being.

In moving out at night
Or spending time with friends of their choice
Women mistake to endure as their freedom
They believe it's the only solution to all the
havoc

The real enfranchisement and exemption
Is letting others know about their personality
That the identity of women is much more
Than they think of them to mould

A mother, sister and so many appearances
She is the one who cares blandly
Please, seek inside your heart for salvation
A real self is hidden within your core
peritoneum

Don't tell the world about your composition
Do something extremely amazing for the
universe
That they themselves kneel down and praise
Rise! Lift! Recognise your self-worth

Beauty

The eyes of a child speak so much,
The tongue of a child, too shy to touch.
I love the most when I'm adored,
A child's beauty lies in her Mom.
As parents, we often fight,
Who will show her love with all their might?
The answer we always find,
Her kisses on our cheeks, so kind.
We've heard it said a thousand times,
'Beauty's in the eyes of the beholder'.
But for me, true beauty is in a child's
innocence – unspoiled and pure.